C000212287

In Daniele Pantano we have found an heir to Czesl[
— John Domini, twice n[

"We sing – because we are lost." Employing a stac
strangely beautiful voices, Daniele Pantano's *Home f*
we cannot bear to reveal lest they shatter the stories ⌐⌐ ⌐⌐ ⌐⌐⌐ ⌐⌐⌐ ⌐⌐⌐⌐⌐
wrongs which haunt us still, maiming our ability to love one another, to be vulnerable again.
The language – always concise, clear, vivid – varies from the brightly lyrical to the darkly fairy-
tale, through to the chilly vocabulary of documentary and bureaucratic lists. The poems may
be bleak in their truths, but it is through these voices, if we have the body, heart and spirit to
be open to their beauty and terror, that we may be blessed with the vision of a more authentic
way to live and love.

— Ian Seed, *The Underground Cabaret*

Daniele Pantano writes something we might call confessional conceptual writing, with its
lyrical listing, forensic fairytales. His poems often present inventive inventories of mysterious
actions in a menacing world, a world of deadly serious playgrounds, playscripts for isolated
dancers. We need them.

His preference for errata and marginalia, his refusal to write the kind of poem "that famous
poets on twitter write these days and publish in *the new yorker*: a poem about tears" does not
preclude lyric poems with the pain of its momentary selfhood, precisely a poem about tears.
His essentially pan-European sensibility finds him toppling in and out of English, finding the
other side of exile in a painful homecoming.

All of this is related in sharply delineated forms, pieced together with a clarity that burns
and shines. We need these poems to relate the complexities of our moment.

— Robert Sheppard, *The English Strain*

Reading *Home for Difficult Children* feels a little like happening on the aftermath of an
investigation, an interrogation, which may also be the crime scene itself: files scattered,
tapes unspooled. Even the titles of these poems – shadowed in parentheses by their own
alternatives, Gestalt switches to other readings – undercut the possibility of any singular
meaning. English is unsettled by German and French, pushed through various mechanisms
and transformations, so that the things it might have resisted saying (both personal and
historical) rise to the surface in unexpected ways: "this other thing / we cannot name pleading
// to speak again." There is a dark pleasure here in the images of ballerinas under interrogation,
of the wrong side of a children's birthday party, "the shrieks of cotton candy and love hearts,"
of poetry itself as a *Rabenmutter*, a bad mother, unleashing onto these pages "the orphans
locked up in our dark playgrounds."

— Helen Tookey, *City of Departures*

One of the poems in *Home for Difficult Children* contains the line *you still cannot find what you
know* – and that's the terrain one travels as one works through this dark, troubled collection.
Pantano's poems contain Georg Trakl's dark forests, Robert Walser's cities and sanatoriums,
Paul Celan's collapsed/condensed interiors, and Andrei Tarkovsky's shrouded landscapes.
These disturbing, moving poems climb over a great deal of 20th century European culture –
often feeling like Super 8 movies of a disappeared world. But here's the thing. It's 2022 – and
in the intensity of their dark light, they also, suddenly, feel terrifyingly contemporary.

— Tim Atkins, *On Fathers < On Daughtyrs*

Also by Daniele Pantano

POETRY

Chiens dans des champs en friche (Editions d'en bas, 2020)

Dogs (Jona Editore, 2020)

14 Poem(a)s (Ediciones Abend, 2019)

Waldeinsamkeit (13) (zimZalla, 2018)

ORAKL (Black Lawrence Press, 2017)

Hunde in verwahrlosten Feldern (Wolfbach Verlag, 2015)

Mass Graves: City of Now (KF&S Press, 2012)

Mass Graves (XIX-XXII) (KF&S Press, 2011)

The Oldest Hands in the World (Black Lawrence Press, 2010)

Panta Rhei (Alpha Beat Press, 2000)

Camera Obscura (Carlyle Press, 1999)

Blue Opium (Carlyle Press, 1997)

Geschlüpfte Kreaturen (Private Publication, 1997)

Blumendürre: Visionen einer Reise (Private Publication, 1996)

ESSAYS, VISUAL, AND CONCEPTUAL LITERATURE

333 (etkcontext, 2022)

Ten Million and One Silences (edition taberna kritika, 2021)

Sinner (TAP Editions, 2021)

Six Essays (aaaa press, 2020)

Kindertotenlieder: Collected Early Essays & Letters & Confessions (Hesterglock Press, 2019)

TRANSLATIONS

Robert Walser: The Poems (Seagull Books, 2022)

Friedrich Dürrenmatt's The Virus Epidemic in South Africa (Centre Dürrenmatt, 2022)

Michael Fehr: super light (Der gesunde Menschenversand, 2020)

Robert Walser: Comedies (Seagull Books, 2018)

Fairy Tales: Selected Dramolettes by Robert Walser (New Directions, 2015)

Oppressive Light: Selected Poems by Robert Walser (Black Lawrence Press, 2012)

The Possible Is Monstrous: Selected Poems by Friedrich Dürrenmatt (Black Lawrence Press, 2010)

In an Abandoned Room: Selected Poems by Georg Trakl (Erbacce Press, 2008)

HOME FOR DIFFICULT CHILDREN

Pantano

swiss arts council

prohelvetia

Supported by a Pro Helvetia Literature Creation Grant.

ISBN: 978-1-915079-94-7 (paperback)
ISBN: 978-1-915079-65-7 (hardback)

Cover designed by Aaron Kent

Edited and typeset by Aaron Kent

Broken Sleep Books   Broken Sleep Books
Rhydwen   Fair View
Talgarreg   St Georges Road
Ceredigion   Cornwall
SA44 4HB   PL26 7YH

Contents

I
RABENMÜTTER (ARS POETICA)   13

II
BIRTH CERTIFICATE (COUNTERQUESTIONS)   17
SATURDAY (LEXICONS)   18
PLACEBO (MERCEDES)   19
TEST PATTERN (OLFACTORY BOYHOOD)   20
THREE HAZELNUTS (CINDERELLA)   22
FAIRY TALE (WITH UNSOLVED MURDER)   23
SEE-SAW (YOUR SECRET POPULARITY)   28
MOTEL (WINDOW)   29
LATE DECEMBER   30
KATZENJAMMER   31

III
CITY OF NOW   35
ICON (FRAGMENT OF A CRUCIFIXION)   36
BIRTHDAY PARTY (BACK OF)   37
BALLERINAS   38
HIDDEN AIRPLANES (SOPHIE PODOLSKI)   40
FOLEY 4:10   41
SUBURBAN BRAINS (BUS STOP)   43
LANDSCAPE WITH RAG (HOW)   44
A PLAY (FOR ONE CHARACTER)   45
THE FUTURE OF STATUES   46

IV
AESTHETIC (CONSTRUCTIVISM)   49
I AM LIKE AN IDIOT (REED & BOWL)   50
ERRATA   51
SUPERCHROM (THAT)   52
THE FATALISTS   53
WE'LL GO DANCING—WE'LL BE SAFE   54
PICTURE (SHOW)   55
TRIBUTE (MINIMALISM)   56
SANITORIUM   57
WALKING (FIGURE)   58

V
CONTRE-JOUR (BURDEN)   61
SAFE HOUSE (FOR LACK OF A BETTER TERM)   62
SPEAKING TO THE CONSUL   63
BETWEEN STATIONS OF THE METRO   64
GEOMETRIES OF EXILE (OR)   65
LIFE (JACKET)   66

SLAPSTICK (H.)   67
STUDY IN SOOT & HYPERTONIC SALINE   68
ARCHIPELAGO: OR ANOTHER RECESSION OVERHEARD [...]   69
LAST VISIT & SUPPER PRIOR TO THE INVASION [...]   70

VI

FUNNY HOW (LASSNIG)   73
MORNING WALK   74
DOPPELGÄNGER   75
SAINT (STRAWBERRY LEMONADE)   76
CHAOS THEORY   77
FALLOW GROUND   78
ELEVATOR (MUSIC)   79
DOMINOES—OPENING   80
EASTERN VILLAGE WITH FACTORY   82
EXIT (POINTS)   83

VII

DEATH OF A MARRIAGE   87
AND MY SON (SPEAKS THE SADDEST LINE)   88
WE FUCK (ALONE)   89
DIVORCE (SOMETHING ARTIFICIAL)   90
STILL LIFE (SELF-PORTRAIT)   91
ANXIETY (ON LIVING SOON)   92
DRAFT 1 (DOMESTIC)   93
URBAN LANDSCAPE PAINTING (WITH VIRUS)   94
REWRITE   95
THIS IS (WE, THE POEM)   97

VIII

HOMECOMING (LANGENTHAL)   101
SIX OBSTACLES   102
SENTENCE (HOUSE)   105
IN AN ABANDONED WAREHOUSE   107
MAMIHLAPINATAPAI   108
LOW-VOICED CONFESSIONS   110
TRANSCRIPTION OF SELECTED MARGINALIA FOUND IN 1983   112
133 WORDS, 133 CIGARETTES [...]   116
VAUDEVILLE   118
TRANSLATION FROM THE GERMAN [...]   119

IX

TWENTY (WITHOUT ENDINGS)   124

ACKNOWLEDGMENTS   127

Home for Difficult Children

Daniele Pantano

For my children Fiona Katharina and Giacomo Daniele
you are what I cannot write

"A red dress flies through a crowd of children."
  — Georg Trakl

I

RABENMÜTTER (ARS POETICA)

I

—lines are lines. are lines. they are not. alone. in the world.—

II

—that's how we will sum up those years.—songs we didn't dance to.

II

BIRTH CERTIFICATE (COUNTERQUESTIONS)

When the investigator arrives, I name him
here I am. I name him motherland. No one
will see you. I have given birth in the mirror.
A tatum, in all likelihood. Or Kokoschka's
sex doll. Ruptured and headless, of course.
Don't we name what we name to understand
what named us? The only truth is how water
speaks to the moon. What are we waiting for?
The more important the man, the sicker his sexuality,
wrote Alma Mahler. No one will answer you.
The committee. Between your questions, us.
Indeed. She wrote, *my fantasy is full of the most*
perverse images of cripples and seeking crippledom.
And did you get what you wanted? You are
never within, never without. Let me, too, be
an invisible act. Compassionate, selfless, yes.
What is between a doll and a pulse, a skin
and a lashing—this newborn and the next?

SATURDAY (LEXICONS)

nevertheless we are
          born in each other's

playgrounds abandoned
          kinder in red-white

wrappers shredded into
          toy-sized once upon

a times and wherevers
          for the golden gummibärchen

communion lined by spillikins
          deep in plasticine dirt

we mount little tikes horses
          and push through blacked-

out windows down country
          lanes misfiring engines

clutch at us feral saints
          a time past propped up

on cinder blocks our wasted mothers
          of foxes your hair still smells

like the summer rain of 1983

PLACEBO (MERCEDES)

—i was the mother. i put the ambulance sirens on the nightstand.—i was gone too. i swept the floor. thrilled at being unidentified.—i started to think once more. about the first shots that struck you. i wasn't sure just then.—i diverted the riot police. i was doing the right thing. i had so little.—i told them. you'd left. i washed my hands. and yours. i heard the doors close.—i wrote their stories. read them on short wave radio. i had enough time to leave.—i didn't notice. our wandering around the city. i got there. i said. let's see.—i sat in the back of your classic mercedes. trembling. i wanted more. i imagined we would forget. where we'd started.—i laughed. i said goodbye. and let them in. i admit. for just a second. everything seemed like. i'd wanted it. to be.—

TEST PATTERN (OLFACTORY BOYHOOD)

1. Pine Tree
2. Ovaltine
3. WD-40
4. Rhubarb
5. White-Out
6. Ammonia
7. Dirty Band-Aid
8. Saliva
9. Yellow Pages
10. Dried Semen
11. 80s Wood Paneling
12. Bicycle Tire
13. Angel's Trumpet
14. Jockstrap
15. Sex Wax
16. Werther's Original
17. Gasoline
18. Pork Sausage
19. Dunhill Red
20. Legos
21. Hustler Magazine
22. Rust
23. Talcum Powder
24. Skateboard
25. Smegma
26. Red Spray Paint
27. Arancini
28. Nivea Hand Cream
29. Taxidermic Moth
30. Leather Racing Gloves
31. Opium by Yves Saint Laurent
32. Cheesecloth

33. Grass-Stained Denim
34. Shoe Polish
35. His Hands
36. Diesel
37. Gangrene
38. Pernod
39. Elmer's School Glue
40. Black Mold
41. Football
42. Steel Butt Plug
43. Chloroform

THREE HAZELNUTS (CINDERELLA)

(1)

you speak. of childhood. so bring your sad horses inside. and tell me. what will you do. to me. again. not in a hush. but in a whisper. twisted and weightless. with the sky like chocolate. while your beasts forgive themselves. treacherously. dancing against. the charred bush.

(2)

how sweet. to grieve. how sweet. to watch your house burn down. never to lock. your splendid doors. again. memory as a body of hulls.

(3)

someday we will. name a new color. again. hide inside its pigment. a rediscovered light.

FAIRY TALE (WITH UNSOLVED MURDER)

—*It's yesterday. And who will remember?*

—You watch the way home for hours.

—Schedules of trains reaching the source of the plot.

—The same day her parents filed a missing person report.

—I swear you can find her name in the margins of this text.

—Of any text.

—It's yesterday.

booklouse—any of various small, often wingless insects of the order *Psocoptera*, which feed on paper and bookbindings.

—*It's yesterday. And who will remember?*

—And so they began to experiment with anniversaries.

—Is that your problem?

—Stepping off the page.

—Black tiptoed resistance.

—Neither distant nor bothered.

—It's yesterday.

pinworm—a parasitic nematode worm, *Enterobius vermicularis*, infecting the colon, rectum, and anus of humans. Children are at high risk of infection.

—*It's yesterday. And who will remember?*

—Years ago something happened.

—Couples promoted into the boundaries.

—Left as sacrifice.

—Like letters on a billboard.

—No point in hanging on any longer.

—It's yesterday.

hookworm—a parasitic blood-sucking nematode worm, *Ancylostoma duodenale* or *Necator americanus*, having hooked mouthparts with which they fasten themselves to the intestinal walls of various animals, including humans. Children are at high risk of infection.

—*It's yesterday. And who will remember?*

—Dead ground re-writing history.

—Dampness. And the same children from the previous poems.

—Remember them. Setting fire to the orphanage.

—Strangling the caretaker with a garden hose.

—Comprehend these sudden phobias:

Anablephobia
Chirophobia
Geliophobia
Menophobia
Kolpophobia

—It's yesterday.

tapeworm—any parasitic ribbon-like flatworm of the class *Cestoda*, having a body divided into many egg-producing segments and lacking a mouth and gut. The adults inhabit the intestines of vertebrates, including humans. Children are at high risk of infection.

—*It's yesterday. And who will remember?*

—But if all is _____

—Was it the year we celebrated the death of our pets?

—The death of our children?

—Born _____

—Raised on expired medicine.

—It's yesterday.

roundworm—any nematode worm, especially *Ascaris lumbricoides*, a common intestinal parasite of man and pigs. Children are at high risk of infection.

—*It's yesterday. And who will remember?*

—From a distance.

—She makes you feel changed for having_____her.

—Most influential child, yes.

—What else is one to do?

—Marks on the back of an envelope:

> The name of this medicine is_____(250mg tablets)
> Do not pass it on to others. It may harm them.
> Possible side effects: unusual bleeding or bruising.
> Other unwanted effects which are more likely to occur are:
> nausea, vomiting, black hairy tongue.

—It's yesterday.

whipworm—any of several parasitic nematode worms of the genus *Trichuris*, esp *T. trichiura*, having a whiplike body and living in the intestines of mammals. Children are at high risk of infection.

—*It's yesterday. And who will remember?*

—The rain stops.

—Advance copies of ____

—The grammar school.

—Inspector Barlach?

—Swiss folktales, myths, legends:

> (titles of tales yet to be translated)

"The Black Water Puck"
"The Shepherd and the Giant"
"The Cat in the Milk Can"
"The Dwarf Wedding"
"The Jealous Blacksmith"
"The Cheated Devil"
"The Shoemaker in the Oven"
"The Little Red Skirt"

—It's yesterday.

SEE-SAW (YOUR SECRET POPULARITY)

—the amusing elegance. the generosity. the youth of solitudes. the orphans locked up in our dark playgrounds. the unexpected warmth stretching like a blanket. the courage of sickness and desire. the stories we tell ourselves.—

MOTEL (WINDOW)

what happened to us at such an hour the postman picks lemons
        and tomatoes en route to the tiniest boxes of lies
the empty school bus delivers our children's terror without blame
        or refusal because the morning light is a fresh bandage
the mother singing to the little girl who is ready for another forgive
        me who does not belong to cruel answers scribbled
somewhere no the morning cigarette is not solitude it's a loss of faith
        and it's not too late to take pleasure in more survival
someone keeps going we all do what would you say
        why do they not dream of our thirst when all we are
is thirsty the catastrophe we confess when we show
        how lucky and forgotten we truly are how the rain
came to destroy us the poor the silent the miracles
        of a lifetime we keep reading and rereading Pozzi:

    and now you want me to tell you the history of birds?

    and now you want me to tell you the history of birds?

    and now you want me to tell you the history of birds?

        we can't hear it all passing over us unclean as we are
every beautiful thing is as painful as everything else

29

LATE DECEMBER

Clearly. Nothing much is happening. Kids continue to wish.
For snow. The rest. For something other than the possible.
Something other than the fog. Settling as thorns. Frozen.
On fences. Winter, in its subtlest arrival, barbs our barriers.
Still. No one misses the ordinary. Not even the blackbirds.
Just as no one, on either side, misses the end of the world.

KATZENJAMMER

Nothing you need to know is still missing. The desired principle in your hands you ought to chase right now.

On one page you don't remember writing "I don't remember."

III

CITY OF NOW

More profound than reason,
More profound than perversion,
Bestiality, does she, determined,
Absorbed, think and connect us,
Larger than a common grave,
The dark trying of her fingers,
Counting these pages?

ICON (FRAGMENT OF A CRUCIFIXION)

—we're throwing it all away. this nowhere. torn from our chests. rushing down the stairs. barricaded hallways. we know perfectly well. why the street kids simply smile. at the lunatic troupe. returning late. to their unexplained deaths. like an autobiography. packed with hope. and modest pride.—we'll clean the rest for you. you'll be safe here. to urinate in the courtyard. play with our broad-chested toys. never mind. the awful stench. drink the bodies of your beloved. her enormous tumor. emerge from this filthy dream. it's waiting for you. around the corner.—

BIRTHDAY PARTY (BACK OF)

Be careful in whose house you speak.
Speaking in pinks or reds or yellows is
a matter of loss. How hard the work,
the bright nakedness you are made of.
Or the cutout of yourself as a child,
an upended prison—two birthmarks
on the small of your back and neither
knows the other's name. The one who
told you everything you know. Why did
the hustler catch you *drowning in orphaned milk*?
Blue plastic tractor Polaroid in the back pocket
of his jeans. Secrets don't believe in magic
or the fate of autonomous door alarms.
It's raining now. And there they are again.
Any minute now. Watch them closely. Still.
Already. It's June. It's time for new pictures.
The shrieks of cotton candy and love hearts.

BALLERINAS

Dancer 1:

—The Home for Difficult Children moved in next door to her.

Dancer 2:

—I saw her madness, strange sister, and chose another.

—Her mouth formed a documentary subject: the city thin as light.

Dancer 3:

—She was interviewed by a pair of twins who spoke "only the insufferable language of the young, the only language that deserves to be saved."

> Two questions:
>
> What is the most human virtue of all? And if there's a song that defies all classification, what would it be?
>
> It goes without saying. Happiness. No, humor or courage. And singing goodbye to one's native tongue.

Dancer 4:

—She developed a sense for when he was coming.

Dancer 5:

—She was more modest than she appeared, she had promised, she told herself quite frankly, she felt drawn, she sang, she received and entertained him, she found herself compelled, she wished, she added in hushed tones, she said, she knuckled under, she began to contemplate vile and wicked things, she called to mind, she looked, she sank, she dragged, she thrust his hands away, she softly, softly walked, she hated him, she sat there, she kept warning him, she didn't even look at him, she gave him the bread, she said something, she called him, she harmonized so well, she confessed to him, she responded, she considered herself, she was deeply immersed, she indeed began, she asked, she proceeded, she was a sort of, she sometimes believed, she might possibly, she was in fact, she was nothing more, she was forced, she might be too, she longed for, she wished to, she appeared, she wept, she did so, she was delicate, she shivered, she was single, she harbored, she didn't know anything, she no longer wanted, she was still, she found herself, she became, she framed, she ran out.

Dancer 6:

—Emaciated: *adjective* free from legal, social, or political restrictions; liberated.

—Abuse: *noun* violent treatment involving sexual assault (someone, esp. a woman or child), esp. on a repeated basis.

Dancer 7:

Brisé, Chaînés, Chassé, Croisé, Écarté, Échappé, Effacé, Fouetté, Plié, Piqué, Porté, Relevé, Retiré, Sauté, Tombé.

HIDDEN AIRPLANES (SOPHIE PODOLSKI)

—it wasn't simple. like people waiting in line.—*it's as simple as that.*—her eyes staring nervously at the ceiling.—the story about the poets and painters. in the kitchen. *it would be wrong to disclose the language.* it repeats itself at random. *the way you tie your shoes.*—and when did you learn to dance to an open provocation? *i'm not here to be stranger than you.* this daughter who wears glasses to fly hidden airplanes.—*but no one has translated any of this.* of this. that is. *in filthy cinemas.* her youth. *the toilet paper in your hand.*—and now that i think about it. *i don't know.* her parents. *you got it wrong.* a kiss on the cheek. *that's easy. the chaos of space shut my mouth.*—the wet nurses. *nothing more to it.*—in her left hand. a magazine. *read me your poems. the one about the poets and painters in the kitchen.*—aren't all names dull and corrupt political acts. to be read. between the lines. like so many others.—a foam mattress. *another page.* the shop on the ground floor.—after the premature sunrise. i promised her. i would live in this blondness. *i can stay here.*—

FOLEY 4:10

Set/Index	Time	Sound
MG-C/129	0:07	Dust falls lightly
MG-C/333	0:14	Tarp cloth, in wind
MG-C/441	0:12	Branch movement, steady
MG-C/002	0:29	Oxygen mask, single breaths
MG-C/134	0:08	Dog footsteps on linoleum
MG-C/205	0:11	Man urinates on the ground
MG-C/415	0:02	Cigarette toss to the ground
MG-C/038	0:05	Metal, creaks and groans, high pitched
MG-C/618	0:02	Paper movement
MG-C/137	0:09	Brush dust off a wall
MG-C/077	0:03	Metal object drops, heavy impact
MG-C/054	0:21	Artifact movement, small
MG-C/330	0:03	Finger down on wood
MG-C/901	0:12	Bedframe, creaks
MG-C/709	0:15	Brush hair
MG-C/842	0:11	Scissors cutting
MG-C/008	0:08	Chewing gum/eating candy

MG-C/256	0:05	Panties, movements, drop
MG-C/470	0:17	Rosary beads movement
MG-C/603	0:14	Grass movement, light
MG-C/802	0:03	Girl kneels on grass
MG-C/054	0:03	Digging in the dirt with hands
MG-C/141	0:04	Fingers bite
MG-C/579	0:11	Shaking something off the body
MG-C/012	0:04	Wood splinters, distant crash on soft surface
MG-C/089	0:02	Skull hits with sharp bone
MG-C/201	0:07	Pin through a bug
MG-C/039	0:04	Heavy exoskeleton cracks
MG-C/098	0:05	Light body falls on leaves
MG-C/111	0:04	Male grunts
MG-C/021	0:02	Licking or sucking fingers or
MG-C/112	0:03	Wipe mouth
MG-C/000	1:02	Ash falls lightly

SUBURBAN BRAINS (BUS STOP)

after Pipilotti Rist

—this lubricious little body. there. with thousands of premonitions—*a blouse. hanging open.* the main news. on vacant streets. past the house fronts. *you can see. what she's doing.* says the forty-year-old. who's just projected christiane f. onto his bedroom wall—*why all this talk about a lifetime of love?*—says the most jarring voice. the chorus of the anointed ones—*but it's not funny.* to anyone else waiting. for the bus. *that feeling you just can't shake.* the thought—that century of the spirit. when you concentrate—crushed—in short. *when you refuse this ragged body.* so many wrongs understood. and not cared for. so many marriages walked out on. without noticing it—they all laugh. *in god we trust. 'cause our saliva is. your diving suit. in the ocean of pain.* —

LANDSCAPE WITH RAG (HOW)

a stone's throw away
       your sisters are dead

too if only devastation
       could sound like sleep-

walking before the day
       you should've left you

told me how to misread
       sleep for a rope a dank

neck a crackling light
       how we're all better

for it how the history
       of the sky remains

as we do open and mis-
       sing how we will forget

the half-forgotten for good
       how by the lakeside your

body unwashed will never be

A PLAY (FOR ONE CHARACTER)

—take off. your shoes. the voice said. and keep walking. ahead. around. through. that theater. you built for her. the messy studio. you promised. the college girls. with freckled arms. balance. signs and borders.—move on. it's the first day of spring. i know. nothing about you.—remember. how much. you loved that smell. that first thick stain. when everything finally made sense. the switchblade. your mother gave you. as a birthday present. to pick your teeth with.—remember the drawn-out film. about empty cars. sleepwalking credits.—for what it's worth. you don't deserve. to be saved.—

THE FUTURE OF STATUES

You are kept awake
By the same names—
There's nothing else.

IV

AESTHETIC (CONSTRUCTIVISM)

it doesn't matter that everybody's ok. you still cannot find what you know. the childhood fever. the butcher kneeling in the black forest. the beasts alone in the flood. burn marks. so it goes. the sun you ate fucking another. a shade sadder than knowing what you know. nobody wants a leak more beautiful than a line. if the sister of bees could only die. you said. for a queen. a choice is always received. a letter as terrible as rats walking on water. a photograph. you turn. as our turn. the operating theater. yet I still listen to you. like a leaf. turned. that will never believe again. a breath. without one word you play raptures. when they do melancholy. attached to a public scandal. this is always the case. last wish. holy again the face that knocks on the door.

I AM LIKE AN IDIOT (REED & BOWL)

His wish: to be
Buried they grasp
The single idea
Wood—a line—
Whatever the promise
Prolongs this silence
A seed calling out
To the river's soft waste

ERRATA

after Tolstoy

Page 04,   line 19:   for *time fails to reach us* read *I sent a message in German*

Page 15,   line 06:   delete semicolon and line after *it's just a matter of theory*

Page 17,   line 10:   for *do not* read *allow us to taste the pomegranates in silence*

Page 22,   line 32:   delete full stop after *be ashamed of our flesh that rages*

Page 38,   line 08:   for *ponder this rope* read *patient and abandoned ululation*

Page 40,   line 25:   for *fury* read *the language in our hands becomes another*

Page 41,   line 12:   insert comma after *children, stills on the cutting-room floor*

Page 49,   line 04:   for *seemingly doubtless* read *frozen and brutal and found*

Page 56,   line 27:   for *our duty to teach others* read *posthypnotic museum*

Page 63,   line 31:   for *shapeless and unformed* read *as though sewn together*

Page 68,   line 15:   delete comma and rest of line after *we were only young*

Page 72,   line 16:   for *breathe for one another* read *breath is a palimpsest*

Page 83,   line 22:   delete dash at beginning of line after *Ausschnitt*

Page 91,   line 03:   for *we will never be as hungry* read *beautiful . . .*

SUPERCHROM (THAT)

that black ice that is your shadow
        or whatever you want to call it
that failed to carry you out of
        that burnt out basement time
and again or father's swollen
        body that floated down the river
with that music you recorded
        on that Agfa Superchrom cassette
that spring you reached mother's
        suicide dream in that Swiss forest
near that flooded riverbank with
        that fisherman hauling that net
of effluvia is the same as that
        annihilation that entered you
when you were still that you
        that boy watching from that hill
above that water on that stolen bike
        with that crown of marshmallows
that Benzedrine smile

THE FATALISTS

for Fiona

Bad thoughts, she says. *Bad thoughts.* Like him when he was her
Age. Six. Seven. Eight. It meant something. He remembers.

Find the stargazer. Find it! She yells. Her little box on the nightstand.

It's summer again. With every year, fear changes into expectation, surprise
Into denial. All the windows are open. Smoke billowing from the trees.

Nature is a disc that never stops spinning, Daddy. He wants her to prove it.

She writes. *The world around me: I'm sleeping in the forest and it is scary to me.*

Why the forest? He waits. *I saw a woman in disguise: I went to the park.*
A woman with a black coat on and a big hat on and she was staring at me and my

Spotted dog. And my feet covered with warts, Daddy? January fields. Black stars.

He thinks. *Have the tigers emerged, Daddy?* They are moving. From chamber
To chamber. In the house built on ice. They smile. You'll see.

It's your brother in the adjacent room. His delicate balalaika snores.

Good night, my love. But who is he to tell her to think of something
Beautiful . . . who is he to tell her that everything is going to be fine?

* Lines in italics were written by Fiona Pantano at age six.

WE'LL GO DANCING—WE'LL BE SAFE

Chämi uff und niän-ä-n-a . You wanted to go so fast . In den Kronen . A muscular contraction . Listen . It takes three beggars . Das ist mein Satz . Being . In den Kronen . In this strange and marvelous state . Sieht keiner denkt keiner . In its other logic . Turns immense . Whether they give us back our megaphones or not . In den Kronen . Was steht in den Kronen . Listen . Ich habe keinen andern . Four in the morning . Der Tanz . How will it look . Listen . In den Kronen . With your escape mechanism . You whisper . Listen . Das ist mein Satz . Others move to stop . What do you want . This is my sentence . No one sees someone thinks . Strange and marvelous . A nurse's nose . Ah, there . From today on it is as we think . How strange to be . In den Kronen . Turns immense . Listen . Another stone . More prizes to be won . Instantly . The hair grows back . In den Kronen . Mechanism . Ein fremdes Wundenmal . But what about the flesh . Discalced . Der Tanz . Don't whisper . We should say . Listen . It is as we think . Sieht keiner denkt keiner . A muscular contraction . This is your sentence . Chämi uff und niän-ä-n-a . Didn't stay still . Dein Wundenmal . Now everyone whispers . In its other logic . You're doing it right . Listen . A sentence is . You whisper . You wanted to go so fast . Strange and marvelous . In den Kronen . Was steht in den Kronen . Give us back our megaphones .

PICTURE (SHOW)

at a certain point
in the famous

film the softness
of language

can be measured
and missed

without ever looking
up to gather what

would be by now
a deliberate thought

a narcoleptic animal
quivers in the cornice

like your madness
the credits fade

as it gets cold all
you see is the red

coupe leaving
amid the ruins

tell yourself night
began as a darkness

inside a mouth

TRIBUTE (MINIMALISM)

—we didn't know we were burning. burning the other day. without the least desire.—the thought of success. in our pockets.—they told us not to sleep. drink stale coffee. that heat sacks weigh more than unhappiness.— yes. we're all damp. sheets on a cot. or by divine recognition.—the infection. like the drug. remained the same. like beauty too. we'd been lucky. studied our dutch angles. in and out of the psychiatric clinic.— the manual. cellular slaughter. they called it minimalism. accuracy.— everything can be recreated.—and you cracked. and hid the cracks. in the void remembered. remembered yourself.—

SANITORIUM

static neon captures
little of what is left

here shattered jaws
strobing "for sale"

against flaxen walls
they resist however

bad it gets (you) have
mere seconds to speak

without fear we could
be no one they warn us

every beginning is a
dry spell that renames itself

WALKING (FIGURE)

—i fled. more than. resumed my stroll. the absence of this. singular character. creeping letters. of the alphabet.—i might as well. go back to. to reading. the explosions. the clock that is not so.—a young man. with grief. and silence. i am not. my grandfather's heart. stalking its prey. that thing dimmed. by the breath of auschwitz. off the ground. beyond the limits.—i am the only person. the one who spoke. struck by. the company of. those who fell silent. it was a brightness. a hand. or something abstract. that boarded up the windows.—i think of this. whenever the dogs lick. the hunter's sweat.—

V

CONTRE-JOUR (BURDEN)

during the siren test
      without a warning

she's the evacuation
      order no one follows

the shock of low voices
      in the cerement of tunnel

light or larvae the immensely
      moving darkness of a nose-

bleed after the only dream
      she can afford finds her

outside rented windows
      as her remains are

added to the chorus:

    science has failed
    heat is life
    time kills

yet sometimes she's simply
      breathing a brave thing

on the horizon the storm
      that forms childlike and hungry.

SAFE HOUSE (FOR LACK OF A BETTER TERM)

If I strip myself of everything — what's left is not

the pressure of the cardboard gun on my mother's temple
or the sharpied note transcribed for bullied fingers
or the shoelace lost and tied to its chilling looseness
or the wordless fatherhood in rows of garden beds
or the family truths on a taped-over VHS cassette
or the rusted hook with cured cuts of madness
or the syringe golden between a set of steel teeth
or the ammonia jar welting a collapsed lung
or the darkness living under other people's names
or the unanswerable question no one ever made use of
or the undoings that are near impossible to trace
or the crease that tempers the notice to resettle

what's left is a pardon — the appetite of an overcast day

SPEAKING TO THE CONSUL

do you have any other complaints
sitting with your overstuffed animals
on-screen like you absent over their shoulders
the extant script falling in and out of sync
the parade passes by the theater
or the suggestion of

it sure looks different the first time
factory kids perished back into the 80s
thinking why you'd still be here
that's how we are it seems
we'll find another answer or complaint
begging and refusing to be consumed

BETWEEN STATIONS OF THE METRO

How wonderfully it all matches the black bough:
Her artificial leg she sways as flesh. Fingers forking
His beard and the thinning images he considers.
A boy's grin held by two cheeks. Fists. Simple
And unprovoked, like our apparitions we share
Each morning, en passant, from crests of departure
To whatever we still believe possible. How silly.
How silly to think we all reemerge as petals—pulled
Loose. Bereft of what kept us from the rain.

GEOMETRIES OF EXILE (OR)

every day we peddle
                    our nameless names

on the sidewalks the boulevards
                    the train stations demanding

attention this other thing
                    we cannot name pleading

to speak again as the crowd
                    watches the idea of a crowd

our labor our soap our echo
                    beyond the tracks a mule

to the south a white pony
                    a farm to the east smoke

our fists or lives written
                    or drawn by a mute child

who makes the color blue
                    scream all night like a voice

or a sky or nothing at all

LIFE (JACKET)

—i put on.
—my pristine.
—charlie isoe face.
—in the mirror.
—of a public restroom.
—no cameras.
—only the needles.
—my gaze.
—patinated by my tongue.
—eyes with no one.
—to watch.
—mother's suicide ring.
—around my neck.
—her panties' isabelline seam.
—pinching my scrotum.
—i dry drown.
—through the door.
—usher beautiful refugee boys.
—across southern borders.

SLAPSTICK (H.)

And the disciple mimes
      Delivering a set of keys.

And this is where he crashed,
      Isn't it? His face there is

Mine. Built in 1843.
      And white. Before black

Milk. The transition(s).
      And the riots only gulls

Remember. And bicker.
      And dance. Some water

Damage. Odd feature unlocked.
      And space now of loose wallpaper.

Our morning's final edition(s).
      And fresh fat boils in the kitchen.

Already nothing.
      And nothing is sweeter

Than a future—a red door
      With three locks and a loose chain.

STUDY IN SOOT & HYPERTONIC SALINE

Nowhere to go from here. But then
There's always a carnival. Beyond
The edge of town. When and where.
Miles from our mephitic place. We
Accept. Guard towers. Mammatus
Clouds. What used to be a bit of home.
A noise in our ears. A black cat reading
An Irish story. They are still there. —
They are. The only animal that knows
It must die. Moored figures . . .
In the interest of safety, passengers are asked
To leave all items unattended. Any attended
Items will be removed by the local . . . the final
Station. Already un-shot photographs are
Yellowed. Strewn with red biohazard bags.
One is clutching his heavy pad of surgical
Papers. (Or is it Braille?) Another whispers
Into a plastic container. About destruction
And Lent. A woman whose voice moves
Forty steps closer: *It's not the mangled feet.*
The poisoned flesh. It's the faces that are haunting.
The denuded girls. The nurses on their fag breaks.

ARCHIPELAGO: OR ANOTHER RECESSION OVERHEARD IN THE PARK

We wear

        The poet's uniform

    Because our mothers

           Are dead

Fishermen on classic

          Thin ice

      Riddled now

           That barbarians

Have dropped

      Their fatal blows

    Against our singular

        Ideogram a schoolgirl

Is hiding behind

           Apocryphal translations

    More credible

            Than our roaring

Salute to helicopters

        Like skylarks

LAST VISIT & SUPPER PRIOR TO THE INVASION ONLY WE KNEW ABOUT

Finally. Dessert. He opened
The shutters and revealed
Everything that would cease
To matter the next day. Alleys
Where men were playing another
Round of chess—accents equally
On time and women parading
Like citrus trees in a market of dates.
Pubs. Songs. Palaces of worship.
No. Not even the orphanage
Or his pregnant wife's glutted breasts
Would matter. My host insisted
I spend my time writing the important,
Not the beautiful. *What else can we do?*
He asked. *Continue,* I answered.
And excused myself. All of it.
Except my uncleared plate:
Lemon wheels and spilled milk.

VI

FUNNY HOW (LASSNIG)

In the body house like gasps
           of breath when life chokes us

a crying a kind of beauty
           stops as you watch

the field or burn down
           that other house of human

voices you once knew
           to remember the edge where

drowning feels like speaking
           somehow or a lullaby undone

at the end of the softest night
           a country road where some-

where something or some-
           one happens again.

MORNING WALK

for Jay Hopler

Today, let me not ponder life or love or
Who fans the flame at the center of all things

Today, let me simply accept the bombinating
Presence of death in everything I see

DOPPELGÄNGER

Back. At the Luxembourg. People watching. For you. I will
Not cleave to the cardinal semblance. Passing the odd-shaped
Lake. Flagging. The remains. After all this time. We mistake
For our past. The smolder of '68 Citröens. Our adulterous
Riots. In these beds of flowering tobacco. *There is no absence
That cannot be replaced*. Your favorite line. I rose against. Today.

SAINT (STRAWBERRY LEMONADE)

here at last the inscrutable city

       is bound to be against you

the grass carries the weight

       of your hunger it can hear

what's nearing a lie that feels

       no guilt when it comes time

you are dancing everywhere

       in your favorite song *all your dreams*

are made of strawberry lemonade naked

       your image in the receding mirror

is what you hide from me things too

       dark like breadcrumbs or horseflies

your mouth the color of memory

       come here you say *no matter what is*

written on your t-shirt (SPITSHINE)

       the whiteout on your finger is

barely dry the self-loading pistol

       in your hot pants you bought

when you were a nineteen-year-old

       saint putting clouds into a glass jar

I hold my breath as I wash your feet

       as the black Mercedes S-Class pulls up

with the quarter moon remind me how

       to erase myself kneeling in this green

CHAOS THEORY

When did you last withstand the deafening cellar light?

When did you last speak of potatoes, the baskets
Of zucchini flowers, onions on wooden shelves?

Fingers dipped in juice? Don't you see?
They've moved on to poplars and birches.

Names spill from their galleries: deciduous shelters.

You, on the other hand, still tend to your fallow garden.
These wounds you fill. These harvests amid brilliant decay.

FALLOW GROUND

your washboard hands
                         raw immaculate cloths

on a line survival spoils
                         a squall's raving assault

not least because you are
                         what didn't and wouldn't

drift from ridge to furrow
                         at long last you burn into

snow racing across a field
                         a shadow close to baptism

the windbreakers won't slip
                         untethered and reclaimed

it's not another panic room
                         a witness to your transience

this moment you fall in love
                         this flesh near an open fire

ELEVATOR (MUSIC)

—the next day. i came here. encouraged. for nothing. for nothing. i'd read.—i listened for stuff. i was sorry for. the first hours spent. back in the old town.—it was all over because. nothing happened. after what'd happened.—her room smelled. like killing time. just smaller. a black city. a little rougher now. that you think about it.— it'll all slow down. i made her promise.—flags and flipped cars. the payphones. behind the tree.—we were simple. in the afternoon.— told each other the news. the aberrant laws of incarnations.— stammered a sketch.—i still had my face. documents. a window.—a switch to turn off the music.—

DOMINOES—OPENING

2–5

This space coaxed out of
Boundaries the rest is

3–6

Fourteen thirty-one eighty-
Seven info cards pullulate

4–4

A major retrospective

2–4

Every twenty minutes
There is your angle

1–2

Your permission to move away
From and through the center

–

Non-space frays all directions

6–6

The artist

1–3

A patter of frontiers

5–6

The story is true that is
What the shirt says

–6

Projected onto a screen

4–5

A giant boy skinny carrying
Bags and a solid hard-on

2–3

By mouth as it was when it began

–1

His wife empty of people

EASTERN VILLAGE WITH FACTORY

Dogs bark in untended fields. Outside, artificial light
Pools the road nobody's died on with men sauntering
The graveyard shift, unafraid to sing alone. I stretch out
And find I married a woman who doesn't care that they
Have picked up the ambrosial bouquet of sex—neatly
Wrapped in tissue paper—at the foot of our bed. She
Welcomes the rabid charge. Anything that reminds her
She belongs to the faint hinterland. She keeps the doors
Unlocked. I say nothing. Men or dogs. There will be no
Other end.

EXIT (POINTS)

this one's a blue storm
in a cracked jar

but there's no rain.

—

this one's a spiral stair-
case in an orchard

but there's no fox.

—

this one's a downtown
bridge of fingers raised

but there's no singing.

—

and now the sounds of a car
crash from the nearby autobahn

but there's no miracle.

—

and now the folds in the sky
made of ammonia and whispers

but there's no mother.

—

and now we re-strip the carcass
the loneliest parts of our bodies

but there's no answer.

—
and now we listen to what
we should have been told

whatever is forbidden lives a hundred times over.

VII

.

DEATH OF A MARRIAGE

another us breaks before us
        somewhere along this road

our stillborn wakes from his
        sleep wind-torn and clinging

to the hitch-hiking doubles
        abandoned by the roadside

rain at last the flash unsexed
        how heavy the soft shoulder

littered with estrangement
        and spike strips like fangs

we dredge what's left
        a spike in every tooth

a tooth in every spike
        we wolf it back down

to where we once were

AND MY SON (SPEAKS THE SADDEST LINE)

I'm holding hands with my feet.

WE FUCK (ALONE)

i still long for. the one time. i split my gut. near the back of my seat. like this.—*do you know. the way back?* the limits of that. which was something. left behind.—if you understand the assassin. whose eyes water incessantly. you will have heard. the story of his grandfather's dog. how it mauled this young boy.—*are you coming. or going?* the silence making. its way. along the possible. the empty. flushed faces. that was. what had been. now we are. driving into the forest. glimpses of a river.—he hands me his feathers. and weapons. bones and carelessness. the holes in his chest. he tells me. his former girlfriend. with whom he shares. an apartment in ljubljana. is in love with me.— eight thousand kilometers away. my wife and children. pass a few small boats. the polaroid shows my body at a burial. the ancient practice—of letting go.

DIVORCE (SOMETHING ARTIFICIAL)

All I want to say is that I am glad to be in this ridiculous melting pot of a body, that I believe Kierkegaard when he says that "love believes everything—and yet is never to be deceived," that my hoarse, distant sound escaped your throat, that the spiral narrative of September's dead children is a faithful hammering, for better or for worse, that we always headed straight for the small part of the night, that Chesterton wrote marriage is "the most dark and daring of sexual excesses," yes, that I remember Diski's "smoking is a love that has never gone wrong, never seen sense," that we changed our familiar dead in airtight canals, that eating scrambled eggs changes the past, that sitting next to you, the impossible, that noise repeated around the table, is a ravishing memory, that Debord's "there have always been artists and poets capable of living in violence" is true, that our voices will fall asleep on the sidewalk, still waiting for the boredom of waiting, that the soul is a mere byproduct of ordinary reality, that, breathless through the city, it wasn't Mike Kelley who said "something artificial—in an artwork, so to speak—needs to be built up, put together in parts, in order to render some of this complexity," that "this artwork would be made of fragments, and it would not conceal its fragmented form," no, and it wasn't you either, whoever you are, that is, I don't remember anything.

STILL LIFE (SELF–PORTRAIT)

There's the sound of a dormant proposition.
There's the sound of a flesh wound.
There's the sound of a perfect memory.
There's the sound of a glass of pink paint.
There's the sound of a rhetorical condition.
There's the sound of a frozen wave.
There's the sound of a toothless smile.
There's the sound of a dull residue.
There's the sound of a half-written equation.
There's the sound of a medicine cabinet.
There's the sound of a bleached veil.
There's the sound of a body reading.
There's the sound of a pear blossom.
There's the sound of a planned self-portrait.
There's the sound of a final wager.
There's the sound of a stubbed-out cigarette.
There's the sound of

ANXIETY (ON LIVING SOON)

soon we know too much and soon it starts again too soon or soon
after as life heads nowhere soon only to rejoin isolation soon for the time
being or the time that is soon as soon as we cannot see the waste soon
adding to oncoming traffic soon we worry about whatever hope is
hopeless the next day soon we see more emergencies in all we have
soon nothing in our world is too soon or heading nowhere soon running
running running like dogs

DRAFT 1 (DOMESTIC)

—my upstairs neighbor is crying. he cries every night. it's just what happens. around here. you know.—i suppose i ought to write a poem. the kind that famous poets on twitter write these days and publish in *the new yorker*. a poem about tears. my neighbor's tears. his empty valise. his shattered sink. and obsessive movements.—the tears that sweat from his life into mine. the bubbling paint on my ceiling. about how i collect his tears. with a sponge. and how some flowers or weeds sprout from the worn floorboards.—and let's not forget salt. plenty of salt. salt for the soup i'm making. what else.—there's a good chance that it's raining outside. of course. that people in the cities beyond the kitchen window are crying too.—no doubt. there'll be oceans of tears. and vast salt flats past the suburbs. and a line about why i don't call the landlord. fix the water damage. or ask my brother. to help me clean up this mess.—lines about how all men are alone. and where our sadness comes from. and where it all goes in the end.—how one thing or another. or something else entirely has carried. no. schlepped us to this wretched house for silent men.—and then the final line. with its soft light of dawn. its soul larger than life. maybe. or just booze and drugs. or soup or whatever. yes. whatever. whatever.—*whatever* was my wife's favorite word.—

URBAN LANDSCAPE PAINTING
(WITH VIRUS)

The giant in his dead wife's negligee walks down Steep Hill.

Our homeless phenomenologists cheer him on.
There's H., S., and M-P. Marginalia. Invisible.

The American poet C. flanked by chlorinated horses
now asks whether he's read any F. Or A. Or K.

She has never hurt me, he says. She read D. She read N.
Listen. Empty. She entered the world.

The children's hospital. Of a dream.
The afterbirth delivered like smoke.

A yearning for form. A true cancellation
of the future. Of all this talking.

Far from my body. The fever's silver crackle.
Tell the truth for as long as it is possible.

The speed of your amnesiac feet don't fool me.
Why stop walking? I've told no one.

I wash and wash my hands. Her negligee. I wash
the growing dark in the lace. I dry it.

This impossibly ruined house.

REWRITE

what is absolute what is accident what is aircraft what is alone what is annealed what is anywhere what is aporia what is apparatus what is appetite what is asylum what is bell what is beneath what is benevolence what is billowing what is birds screaming what is blunder what is bone-colored what is born what is boundlessness what is brimming what is bruised what is brush what is bullet what is buried what is butter what is buzzing what is canoe what is casing what is chorus what is cities what is cold rain what is common what is conductor what is contemporaneity what is contraption what is conviction what is countless what is coverage what is cradle what is crowd what is desire what is detaching what is determinism what is dimness what is dirty what is disinterest what is distant what is ditto what is dream what is drenched what is efficient what is electroshock what is elegy what is expectation what is exquisite what is father what is feared what is ferry what is flaccidity what is flicker what is flint what is foreseeable what is form what is formalism what is formulaic what is frantic what is gate what is glitter what is grammar what is grinning what is half-forgotten what is hand what is healthy what is hearing what is hearth what is herding what is historical what is hooded what is human what is inertia what is ingénue what is inward what is kingfisher what is knotted what is lapse what is left what is lightning what is lingering what is livestock what is lunacy what is luring what is machine what is maggot what is marigold what is mathematical what is measure what is mechanical what is milk-sour what is misstep what is mollusk what is monotonous what is moonlight what is moss what is mother what is nameless what is newborn what is newsboy what is nimbus what is nowhere what is oil what is optic what is other what is paint what is paper what is performance what is perished what is phenomenon what is pictorial what is pileup what is pill what is polluted what is praise what is prepared what is prototype what is proximity what is pull what is quivering what is ragweed what is rapture what is raw what is razor what is release what is relentless what is remembered what is rigid what is rising water what is riverbank what is root and orchard what is scissors what is sediment what is sewer what is shoulder what is sky what is slipped what is small tongue what is snow what is soil what is somewhere what is spinning what is spreading what is steam what is storm-tossed what is stripped what is sublingual what is surplus what is swallowed what is theater what is the top of the page what is treacherous what is passing what is pattern what is power what is queue what is taken what is teargas what is teeming what is tension what is transmutable what is trench what is triumphant what is tug what is uneven what is uninhibited what is unnamed what is unperceived what is unrequited what is veil what is wanted what is war what is what what is whisper what is wild what is winter song what is within what is whole what is workbook what is woven what is zero what still is

THIS IS (WE, THE POEM)

the trenches
we long for

and walk and call
back all morning

winter's simple
union the sick

finish together
we share what

we cannot hold
cannot fall apart

VIII

HOMECOMING (LANGENTHAL)

The afternoon bell peals the children out of school.

They say it's great to see you after all these years.

You can't look at them. But you believe them.

The missing parents are wading through the rust.

You can't make yourself believe in the end of winter.

Back in the eighties, the papers called this place a *Neonazinest*.

Clear signs. Several cats have been laid out upon a tarp.

Porcelain bowls. Twigs pointing toward the birdbath.

There are no spontaneous protests going on anywhere.

On March 13, your mother shot herself in the head.

The names of the rivers keep changing. A downpour.

Where are the birds? A lifting and flying above the landfill.

Nearby, time is running out. You'd better stay here.

A Tamil man hung from the streetlight. A murmuration.

A golden flag with three rivers. There is so much to lose.

Far from here a perfect Klee sky. A handful of dark ash.

It is March 14. The indispensable and necessary.

There's a mute crowd coming from the other room.

You are the crowd coming from the other room.

SIX OBSTACLES

I

SWISS CIVILIAN CAMPS: including Aarau, Bad Schauenburg, Campo di Lavoro (near Locarno), Cossonay, Fallanden, Felsberg, Hausernmoos, Inkwil, Kemleten, Langenbruck, Lausanne, Les Avants, Leysin, Rheinfelden, Schaffhausen, Sumiswald, Zurich.

SWISS MILITARY CAMPS: including Bettenhausen, Elgg, Ellikon Thur, Langnau, Lutzelfluh, Matzingen, Molondin, Zollikon.

II

Zum anderen Geschlecht fühlte ich mich schon sehr früh hingezogen. Die Stellen, die mich am meisten interessierten, waren die schwärzesten.

Nr. 208, *Landschaft XV*, 1972-73
Acryl auf Papier/Holz
70 x 100 cm

Nr. 219, *Landschaft XX*
Acryl auf Papier/Holz
70 x 100 cm

Nach den 120 Tagen von Sodom, 1968
Transcop
21 x 24 cm

Nr. 232, *Passage XXIV*
Acryl auf Karton/Holz
100 x 70 cm

Back to Mother, 1986
Original Steinlithografie, einfarbig, 3, Zustand
57 x 46 cm

III

Claimant, born on 5 November 1934 in Austria, was denied entry into Switzerland in late 1942. Claimant attempted to enter Switzerland with a group of children at the French-Swiss border. Upon her arrival in Switzerland, claimant was immediately separated from the other members of her group, who were deported and perished, and placed in an orphanage. Claimant states the police beat the children in the group and shaved th9

IV

. . . the Swiss chief of police suggested to the Germans the placing of the J on Jewish passports . . .

WF: *I have not spoken of this for fifty years. But I am convinced the Swiss are guilty of terrible crimes.*

BB: *Ten other children from my French children's home crossed the border but were sent back by the Swiss border guards, straight into the arms of the Germans.*

. . . it is our duty to take children with us, to remove them from their environment, if necessary by robbing or stealing them . . .

V

Some of the flutings appear high up on the walls and ceilings, in every chamber, simple lines, shapes, crude outlines of faces, a specific space for them, by children between the ages of three and seven, with many paintings believed to be the work of an eight-year-old girl, it's impossible to tell whether the flutings were made for play or ritual.

VI

J. L., 2006
Wax, epoxy, wood, metal and showcase
197 x 181 x 80 cm

Pascale, 2003-4
Wax, horsehair, epoxy and wood
140 x 50 x 45 cm

Jelle Luipaard, 2004
Wax, iron, epoxy and wood
174 x 36 x 64 cm

Lost II, 2007
Horse skin, epoxy, metal and wood
98 x 151.5 x 164 cm

We Are All Flesh, 2009
Wood, wax, polyester, steel
105 x 110 x 203 cm

SENTENCE (HOUSE)

finally to be touched
      my mother says is to swallow

the sentence ahead
      of you at a distance she used

to stand outside
      like a man panicked and bruised

and never looking back
      at the reader counting the number

of syllables for lives lived
      with and slaughtered if you want

to know trust in what
      you see in the cellar your hands

the enemy you wished for
      is what you wanted she says this

concentration of knowledge
      without grief life is a fatal success

and there's no time to depart
      back into your luminous shackles

profound as a window shut
      by tears that's it for the time being

I reach for words like honey
      on her lips and no one walks in

the front door but a question
        what goes on the other side

of the sentence mother
        the first letter I could have written

IN AN ABANDONED WAREHOUSE

for Franz Wright

Philosophy failed!

The banner no one could read pronounced.

MAMIHLAPINATAPAI

1.

["they're seated. and earned their degrees in art history. they walk toward the dimly lit corridor"]

2.

["in other words, the logic of small satisfactions mobilizes its subjects toward a critique of our return to the old and new conditions of production. there's always a true enemy, a secretary who knows about the difficult work of changing a light bulb"]

1.

["revolutionary change, thousands of cardboard domes, mutilated bodies, spontaneous echoes and outbursts, smoking or drinking, to limit, to stand up, something that happens to those in the know, guilty and starving, what is money actually the root of, this performance, this property, these charges further confirmed, some hidden message, return to normal, sudden attacks, a to b"]

2.

["i sleepwalk the benzedrine dogs and return home empty-handed. i asked if he could have a few words with me, i mean literally. i'm thinking of the way showing no sign of emotion halts the trains in their tracks— or makes them drown in the inhaler's patented blue"]

1/2.

["it is this that hinders the passerby from complete surrender. the iron cast sculpture in the yard. the swing, garbage cans, barking dogs. the image of giant worms consuming your life. but your legs won't halt. driven by a madness that grows out of the television screen. they continue to run without discretion. without hesitance"]

LOW-VOICED CONFESSIONS

—A city.

—More streets *hanging in the abyss.*

—Somewhere south.

—And a black donkey buried in its public park.

—(For years of service.)

—(Years as a friend.)

—Yes, but we mustn't blame the children.

—They demanded it.

—Blame the *two greatest painters of the twentieth century.*

—*Who weren't even forty when Columbus discovered America.*

—*(One classic, eternal.)*

—*(The other, modern, always, like a pile of shit.)*

—The snail climbs the stalk.

—A moment later past the city walls.

—Dirt road to a neighborhood of silos.

—And irrigation ditches, not asylums or prisons.

—Someone has written PARADOX on one of the silos, we think.

—(Or perhaps it is more accurate to say someone has whispered it into the ground.)

—Not far from another ditch.

—Not far from another tasteful confession.

—(He likes to "bite and pluck their nipples like a bass guitar.")

—The children are listening.

—Black donkeys are German motorcycles.

—We learn to lower our voices and ignore the almost visible.

—As we grow up.

—As we realize the snail: a sniper climbing a silo.

—The painters are prepared to testify.

—*Eating things alive. That's what we do.*

—Blame the detectives.

—Exhibit #1(c):

—(Something mute steps out of a neighborhood.)

TRANSCRIPTION OF SELECTED
MARGINALIA FOUND IN 1983

p. 14

the blue czars
soon realized
how to manipulate
the rain

p. 15

ready to follow
the southern boundaries
of energy

p. 17

I cannot see the difference between hunger
and feasts

p. 19

drawing the shadow on
an insect body
that like a machine
is trying to adjust itself

p. 44

it is the muscle that constructs the four triangles

p. 57

The surreal basement of the purple

house

The white stain on dark trousers
The crime

p. 61   I do not recall the taste of youth

p. 67   a woman lowers her skirt

         we are moving faster

p. 68   without a safety net
         I read the border
         you rise

p. 77   meet the hierarchy of scavengers
         they appease us with alchemy

p. 78   by midnight rivers
         by post-menstrual academies

p. 80   they recover rapidly
         acutely aware of their surroundings

         just two seconds

         they slammed into the wall behind me

p. 85   they placed the tangerine tumor on her chest

p. 96   moments after the lecture I will
         destroy myself

p. 100   the blood of Christ, the cheap wine
                they will be injecting
                in a dark corner of my paradise

p. 105   the senescent baby faces
                are still playing the silent ball game

p. 109   fear is a source of constant amusement

p. 110   genitals dipped in blood

                aroused astral monastery

p. 113   beautiful morning

                child's death

p. 114   he is as specialized as an insect
                for the performance of some inconceivably
                vile function

                centipede cancer

p. 119   the machine is served
                he is a writer

p. 120   perhaps he died

114

p. 136   chaos enables rejuvenated
                anomalies to penetrate the reflections

p. 168   out here memories are two seconds
                shorter and the girls yell
                when they're done

133 WORDS, 133 CIGARETTES (GAULOISES CAPORAL, NON–FILTER)

25 December

novitiate	capsule	doll	benzene
mugshot	ecraseur	[ ]	pregenital
materiality	pulpwood	napthalene	Dragoman
leach	telltale	manacle	rubella
stuva	thymos	Kindertotenwald	

26 December

	tradition	gonorrhea	intersubjectivity
tenant	mucus	methoprene	triskelion
production	acheronta	radical	paraphilia
pearl	cremaster	bisque	restraint
infectivity	[ ]	plow	Nachtgesang

27 December

scarificator	maltitol	jouissance	cloud
vector	pyrrhic	ashlar	roleplay
partition	Ehrfurcht	injection	unwritten
you	arsenic	ritual	matryoshka
silk	Nintendo	allegory	

28 December

pale-skinned	rodeo	type	assoluto
inviolable	enema	suitable	Gretel
host	Bruyckere	polonium	login
harness	confection	protein	teddy
zersprechen	core	multiculturalist	

29 December

	evidentials	sesame	gamete
iconoclast	sack	architect	melancholia
nephrotic	raw	hopscotch	hazard
tiara	ammonia	découvrez	ram
clay	orgasm	necrophilia	Kulturarbeit

30 December

symptomal	cedar	taffy	progenitor
lucidity	subsumed	[ ]	trunk
cadmium	barnslig	trephine	Rapunzel
formica	capitalist	tissue	apotheosis
cosmetic	rectum	dissimulate	

31 December

	flunitrazepam	edifice	nickel
Scarlatina	glare	leitmotif	void
Rotkäppchen	conkers	defututa	puck
spöka	fetishism	susurrus	transgenic
sottotitolata	hymen	purifies	obsolescence

VAUDEVILLE

See the butcher's son lose faith in his knives.

See the worn dock line chafe against the pier.

See the scholar drag her desk into the woods.

See the finger cramp the penultimate étude.

See the grocer highlight his name on the front page.

See the truant child decide on a different shortcut.

See the seamstress enter the building for the last time.

See the survivor hesitate before a shop window.

See the common medlar drop of its own accord.

See, once again, the knives in the porcelain sink.

TRANSLATION FROM THE GERMAN OF SEVENTY-EIGHT EARLY NOTES FOR A BIOGRAPHY OF AN UNKNOWN SWISS POET

1: "I knew him when he still considered himself a Futurist." **2:** Swiss father, carpenter. **3:** Mother, nursing aide (1868–1912). **4:** Born in Burgdorf, Canton of Bern (1889).

5: Followed his parents' advice, plump yet handsome. **6:** Accident at age nine, fell from a third-story window.

7: Studied philosophy and literature at the University of Zurich. **8:** Abandoned, static.

9: (illegible) **10:** It was the wrong year to offer Tzara his manifesto.

11: "You have to hear, be read as being (about) collective movement, courageous, his brother acknowledged" (from *Speed-Bird*,

p. 156). **12:** Dropped out and disappeared in 1911.

13: This is all about timing.

14: Too early for Nabokov (1899–1977). **15:** It sat there for years. **16:** Maybe Chaplin (1889–1977).

17: His cousin discovered him on the Rue Saint-Cannat in Marseille. **18:** Something about a patent for an electromagnetic device (Federal Office for Intellectual Property, Bern, 1908).

19: I'm unable to answer that question here.

20: Don't forget his mother, who took her own life.

21: What made him a mark: his thorn stick à la Du Fu (712–770). **22:** Why not the University of Bern? **23:** Pistol, in the woods, near Melchnau. **24:** Of course he's Swiss. **25:** —Ask Fritz how far I should go with this—.

26: A man, a bag (include only picture).

27: JJ, Wednesday, 5 April 1916, Seefeldstrasse 54. **28:** "Speech and its taste of exile and homeland" (from *Speed-Bird*,

p. 12).   **29:** So he decided not to go through with it (1919).
30: Information

on early childhood spent with an uncle? Or family friend.
31: Speed Poems, he called them.   **32.** His flat, however,
was always left unlocked.

33: "All you heard when you opened the door was music."
34: Birds.

35: That's what he wrote about.   **36:** The
case is exemplary, paradigmatic even.

37: Traveled and conducted experiments (draw
map).   **38:** (illegible)

39: He wanted to buy that summerhouse Nietzsche wrote in,
Sils-Maria, visit Mount Athos.

40: A planned trip to Mexico with a Latin American poet.
41: It wasn't González Martínez.   **42:** But nobody gave
a shit.   **43:** Once she (1900–1983) was still young he kept
fucking her.   **44:** She kept quiet, no letters, but the diary.

45: His first collection sold 33 copies (*Speed-Bird*, 1909).
46: On recycled materials.   **47:** Nothing offensive,
though.   **48:** "It was too soon too late" (interview with friend
and printer, Lausanne).

49: Find civil record — 1918.

50: Several unpublished essays on the Sàmi people (found in
1979).

51: Chapter 4 . . . time and activities in Germany (February
1941–March 1943).   **52:** (This is the sensitive stuff!?)

53: There were others: Isabelle
Eberhardt (1877–1904), Peider Lansel (1863–1943),
Blaise Cendrars (1887–1961),

Maurice Chappaz,
Ullmann (1884–1961), Walser (1878–1956), Albert
Steffen (1884–1963), Alfonsina Storni (1892–1938), Paul Klee,
Friedrich Dürrenmatt.

54: JJ, Saturday, 11 January 1941,
Schwesternhaus zum Roten Kreuz, last meeting.   **55:** The
neighbors used to tell his children — Alois (1924–1941), Damaris
(1927–1962?) — their father should keep the dog from barking.
56: He was the one who fought Jack Johnson (1878–1946),

forget Lloyd! Célan   **57:** According to some (night with

[uncanny resemblance]
in Neuchâtel [impossible]).   **58:** Another   one   with
Hemingway, also impossible.   **59:** (1891–1975) Mother's voice
was "very formal."

                        60: "A matriarch."

       61: —I'm not entirely sure she would've liked that
designation—.   **62:** French, English, a bit of Italian and, to my
surprise, Romansh.

              63: Couldn't stand her anymore.   **64:** They agreed
to return his passport (1955).

                     65: Red Citroën DS (1956).   **66:**
He loved the stutter of that engine.

       67: "The whole room stuffed its mouth with vomit, the
sermon"
(from *Speed-Bird*, p. 42).

                        68: (illegible)
              69: Notebooks #3, 8, 14.

       70: Note from Borges—new thoughts on Schopenhauer.
71: "He came to see me off at the station."   **72:** London,
Barcelona, Paris, back to Zurich.

       73: Rage and madness and literature.
74: "Then he hailed a taxi."

       75: "So poetry is what it is."   **76:** Our story ends with
a meeting (1967).

       77: The mass grave.   **78:** "And we endure, amid seas of
silence, bored to death" (from *Speed-Bird*, p. 72).

IX

TWENTY (WITHOUT ENDINGS)

1. You are saved in a stone house closing in on you.

2. Learn to play the melody you've been given.

3. At last, untie the slipping noose, the weight.

4. Build a kite. Let the world spot its reasons for war.

5. The murderous dregs in the double barrels.

6. We desire—because we suffer.

7. The river or blood running through town.

8. This is a child. This is a sniper. This is a metaphor.

9. If only I could tell you the alley is more than its dumpster fire.

10. Try not to erase the lines: slivers of grammar.

11. We sing—because we are lost.

12. Go south with the migrant birds in your throat.

13. Empty your manifesto: what books taught you.

14. And then, nothing but muscle memory. Lust.

15. Watch the boxcars: vain and pointless.

16. The milkman will bottle the names of the dead.

17. *I don't know you* is your mother tongue.

18. *Tell me* is another way to say *you are flesh*.

19. If you read this again, remember what you wanted.

ACKNOWLEDGMENTS

Grateful recognition is made to the editors and staff of the following journals and literary periodicals in which many of these poems first appeared, sometimes in earlier versions: *The Adirondack Review, antithesis* (University of Melbourne), *Adjacent Pineapple, Bayou Magazine, The Black Market Re-View* (Edge Hill University), *Can We Have Our Ball Back?, Cleaves Journal, The Cortland Review, disClosure* (University of Kentucky), *Dreginald, Ecloga* (University of Strathclyde), *Evergreen Review, Great Works Magazine, harana poetry, Härter, Jacket Magazine, The Mailer Review, Plume, Poetenladen, Poetry London, Poetry Salzburg Review* (University of Salzburg), *Sargasso Magazine, Shipwrights* (Malmö University), *Versal, Verse Daily, The White Whale Review, The Wolf, X-Peri, 3:AM Magazine,* and *32 Poems Magazine.*

Some of these poems have appeared in the following anthologies: *EUROPOE* (University of Kingston Press, 2019), *Morgana-Beat Anthologie* (Morgana Verlag, Germany, 2007), *Poetic Voices Without Borders* (Gival Press, 2009), *Sculpted: Poetry of the Northwest* (North West Poets, 2013), *Vile Products* (Sad Press, 2013), and *Wretched Strangers: Transnational Poetries* (Boiler House Press, University of East Anglia, 2018).

A number of these poems were included in the following chapbooks: *Mass Graves (XIX–XXII)* (KF&S Press, 2011) and *Mass Graves: City of Now* (KF&S Press, 2012).

Deepest gratitude to Aaron Kent for his faith in this book. Thanks to everyone at Broken Sleep Books. Thanks also to my current and former students at the University of South Florida, Florida Southern College, Edge Hill University, and the University of Lincoln.

Thanks to the Swiss Arts Council Pro Helvetia for their support and a generous Literature Creation Grant.

For their valued criticism and lasting friendship, I am inexpressively grateful to James Byrne, Chris Dows, James Reidel, Victor Peppard, Nicholas Samaras, Gregory Smith, and Franz Wright. Last, and most important, I wish to thank my children for their unceasing love, support, and encouragement.

LAY OUT YOUR UNREST